CHILDREN'S FAVORITE ACTIVITY SONGS

Take Me Out to the Ball Game

Distributed by The Child's World®
1980 Lookout Drive • Mankato, MN 56003-1705
800-599-READ • www.childsworld.com

Acknowledgments
The Child's World®: Mary Berendes, Publishing Director
The Design Lab: Kathleen Petelinsek, Design

Library of Congress Cataloging-in-Publication Data
Norworth, Jack.
 Take me out to the ball game / lyrics by Jack Norworth ; illustrated by
Amy Huntington.
    p. cm.
 ISBN 978-1-60954-294-8 (library bound: alk. paper)
1. Children's songs, English–United States–Texts. [1. Baseball—Songs and
music. 2. Songs.] I. Huntington, Amy, ill. II. Title.
 PZ8.3.N855Tak 2011
 782.42—dc22
 [E]   2010032430

Printed in the United States of America in Mankato, Minnesota.
December 2010
PA02074

ILLUSTRATED BY AMY HUNTINGTON

Take me out to the ball game.

Take me out
with the crowd.

Buy me some peanuts
and Cracker Jack,
I don't care if
I never get back.

9

Let me root, root, root
for the home team—
if they don't win it's a shame.

11

For it's one, two, three strikes,
"You're out!" at the old ball game.

SONG ACTIVITY

Take me out to the ball game.
Take me out with the crowd.

 (Sway from side to side.)

Buy me some peanuts and Cracker Jack,
I don't care if I never get back.

 (Shake head from side to side on "never.")

Let me root, root, root for the home team—

 (Pump your fist in the air each time you say "root.")

if they don't win it's a shame.

 (Shrug your shoulders on the word "shame.")

For it's one, two, three strikes,

 (Show the numbers "1," "2," and "3," with your
 fingers when you say the numbers.)

"You're out!" at the old ball game.

BENEFITS OF NURSERY RHYMES AND ACTIVITY SONGS

Activity songs and nursery rhymes are more than just a fun way to pass the time. They are a rich source of intellectual, emotional, and physical development for a young child. Here are some of their benefits:

❀ Learning the words and activities builds the child's self-confidence—"I can do it all by myself!"

❀ The repetitious movements build coordination and motor skills.

❀ The close physical interaction between adult and child reinforces both physical and emotional bonding.

❀ In a context of "fun," the child learns the art of listening in order to learn.

❀ Learning the words expands the child's vocabulary. He or she learns the names of objects and actions that are both familiar and new.

❀ Repeating the words helps develop the child's memory.

❀ Learning the words is an important step toward learning to read.

❀ Reciting the words gives the child a grasp of English grammar and how it works. This enhances the development of language skills.

❀ The rhythms and rhyming patterns sharpen listening skills and teach the child how poetry works. Eventually the child learns to put together his or her own simple rhyming words— "I made a poem!"

ABOUT THE ILLUSTRATOR

Amy Huntington is an artist and children's-book illustrator. She lives in Vermont with her husband, two cats, fifteen hens, one rooster, one tilapia fish, and two sheep.